RENT RECEIPT BOOK

Receipt

Name	Date

DESCRIPTION OF ITEMS/SERVICE	AMOUNT
TOTAL	

RECEIVED BY ______________________

Receipt

Name	Date

DESCRIPTION OF ITEMS/SERVICE	AMOUNT
TOTAL	

RECEIVED BY ______________________

Receipt

Name	Date

DESCRIPTION OF ITEMS/SERVICE	AMOUNT
TOTAL	

RECEIVED BY ______________________

Receipt

Name	Date

DESCRIPTION OF ITEMS/SERVICE	AMOUNT
TOTAL	

RECEIVED BY ______________________

Receipt

Name	Date

DESCRIPTION OF ITEMS/SERVICE	AMOUNT
TOTAL	

RECEIVED BY ______________________

Receipt

Name	Date

DESCRIPTION OF ITEMS/SERVICE	AMOUNT
TOTAL	

RECEIVED BY ______________________

Receipt

Name	Date

DESCRIPTION OF ITEMS/SERVICE	AMOUNT
TOTAL	

RECEIVED BY ____________________

Receipt

Name	Date

DESCRIPTION OF ITEMS/SERVICE	AMOUNT
TOTAL	

RECEIVED BY ____________________

Receipt

Name	Date

DESCRIPTION OF ITEMS/SERVICE	AMOUNT
TOTAL	

RECEIVED BY ____________________

Receipt

Name	Date

DESCRIPTION OF ITEMS/SERVICE	AMOUNT
TOTAL	

RECEIVED BY ______________________________

Receipt

Name	Date

DESCRIPTION OF ITEMS/SERVICE	AMOUNT
TOTAL	

RECEIVED BY ______________________________

Receipt

Name	Date

DESCRIPTION OF ITEMS/SERVICE	AMOUNT
TOTAL	

RECEIVED BY ______________________________

Receipt

Name	Date

DESCRIPTION OF ITEMS/SERVICE	AMOUNT
TOTAL	

RECEIVED BY ______________________

Receipt

Name	Date

DESCRIPTION OF ITEMS/SERVICE	AMOUNT
TOTAL	

RECEIVED BY ______________________

Receipt

Name	Date

DESCRIPTION OF ITEMS/SERVICE	AMOUNT
TOTAL	

RECEIVED BY ______________________

Receipt

Name	Date

DESCRIPTION OF ITEMS/SERVICE	AMOUNT
TOTAL	

RECEIVED BY ______________________

Receipt

Name	Date

DESCRIPTION OF ITEMS/SERVICE	AMOUNT
TOTAL	

RECEIVED BY ______________________

Receipt

Name	Date

DESCRIPTION OF ITEMS/SERVICE	AMOUNT
TOTAL	

RECEIVED BY ______________________

Receipt

Name	Date

DESCRIPTION OF ITEMS/SERVICE	AMOUNT
TOTAL	

RECEIVED BY ______________________

Receipt

Name	Date

DESCRIPTION OF ITEMS/SERVICE	AMOUNT
TOTAL	

RECEIVED BY ______________________

Receipt

Name	Date

DESCRIPTION OF ITEMS/SERVICE	AMOUNT
TOTAL	

RECEIVED BY ______________________

Receipt

Name	Date

DESCRIPTION OF ITEMS/SERVICE	AMOUNT
TOTAL	

RECEIVED BY ______________________

Receipt

Name	Date

DESCRIPTION OF ITEMS/SERVICE	AMOUNT
TOTAL	

RECEIVED BY ______________________

Receipt

Name	Date

DESCRIPTION OF ITEMS/SERVICE	AMOUNT
TOTAL	

RECEIVED BY ______________________

Receipt

Name	Date

DESCRIPTION OF ITEMS/SERVICE	AMOUNT
TOTAL	

RECEIVED BY ______________________

Receipt

Name	Date

DESCRIPTION OF ITEMS/SERVICE	AMOUNT
TOTAL	

RECEIVED BY ______________________

Receipt

Name	Date

DESCRIPTION OF ITEMS/SERVICE	AMOUNT
TOTAL	

RECEIVED BY ______________________

Receipt

Name	Date

DESCRIPTION OF ITEMS/SERVICE	AMOUNT
TOTAL	

RECEIVED BY ______________________

Receipt

Name	Date

DESCRIPTION OF ITEMS/SERVICE	AMOUNT
TOTAL	

RECEIVED BY ______________________

Receipt

Name	Date

DESCRIPTION OF ITEMS/SERVICE	AMOUNT
TOTAL	

RECEIVED BY ______________________

Receipt

Name	Date

DESCRIPTION OF ITEMS/SERVICE	AMOUNT
TOTAL	

RECEIVED BY ______________________

Receipt

Name	Date

DESCRIPTION OF ITEMS/SERVICE	AMOUNT
TOTAL	

RECEIVED BY ______________________

Receipt

Name	Date

DESCRIPTION OF ITEMS/SERVICE	AMOUNT
TOTAL	

RECEIVED BY ______________________

Receipt

Name	Date

DESCRIPTION OF ITEMS/SERVICE	AMOUNT
TOTAL	

RECEIVED BY ____________________

Receipt

Name	Date

DESCRIPTION OF ITEMS/SERVICE	AMOUNT
TOTAL	

RECEIVED BY ____________________

Receipt

Name	Date

DESCRIPTION OF ITEMS/SERVICE	AMOUNT
TOTAL	

RECEIVED BY ____________________

Receipt

Name	Date

DESCRIPTION OF ITEMS/SERVICE	AMOUNT
TOTAL	

RECEIVED BY ______________________________

Receipt

Name	Date

DESCRIPTION OF ITEMS/SERVICE	AMOUNT
TOTAL	

RECEIVED BY ______________________________

Receipt

Name	Date

DESCRIPTION OF ITEMS/SERVICE	AMOUNT
TOTAL	

RECEIVED BY ______________________________

Receipt

Name	Date

DESCRIPTION OF ITEMS/SERVICE	AMOUNT
TOTAL	

RECEIVED BY ______________________

Receipt

Name	Date

DESCRIPTION OF ITEMS/SERVICE	AMOUNT
TOTAL	

RECEIVED BY ______________________

Receipt

Name	Date

DESCRIPTION OF ITEMS/SERVICE	AMOUNT
TOTAL	

RECEIVED BY ______________________

Receipt

Name	Date

DESCRIPTION OF ITEMS/SERVICE	AMOUNT
TOTAL	

RECEIVED BY ______________________

Receipt

Name	Date

DESCRIPTION OF ITEMS/SERVICE	AMOUNT
TOTAL	

RECEIVED BY ______________________

Receipt

Name	Date

DESCRIPTION OF ITEMS/SERVICE	AMOUNT
TOTAL	

RECEIVED BY ______________________

Receipt

Name	Date

DESCRIPTION OF ITEMS/SERVICE	AMOUNT
TOTAL	

RECEIVED BY ______________________________

Receipt

Name	Date

DESCRIPTION OF ITEMS/SERVICE	AMOUNT
TOTAL	

RECEIVED BY ______________________________

Receipt

Name	Date

DESCRIPTION OF ITEMS/SERVICE	AMOUNT
TOTAL	

RECEIVED BY ______________________________

Receipt

Name	Date

DESCRIPTION OF ITEMS/SERVICE	AMOUNT
TOTAL	

RECEIVED BY ______________________

Receipt

Name	Date

DESCRIPTION OF ITEMS/SERVICE	AMOUNT
TOTAL	

RECEIVED BY ______________________

Receipt

Name	Date

DESCRIPTION OF ITEMS/SERVICE	AMOUNT
TOTAL	

RECEIVED BY ______________________

Receipt

Name	Date

DESCRIPTION OF ITEMS/SERVICE	AMOUNT
TOTAL	

RECEIVED BY ______________________

Receipt

Name	Date

DESCRIPTION OF ITEMS/SERVICE	AMOUNT
TOTAL	

RECEIVED BY ______________________

Receipt

Name	Date

DESCRIPTION OF ITEMS/SERVICE	AMOUNT
TOTAL	

RECEIVED BY ______________________

Receipt

Name	Date

DESCRIPTION OF ITEMS/SERVICE	AMOUNT
TOTAL	

RECEIVED BY ______________________

Receipt

Name	Date

DESCRIPTION OF ITEMS/SERVICE	AMOUNT
TOTAL	

RECEIVED BY ______________________

Receipt

Name	Date

DESCRIPTION OF ITEMS/SERVICE	AMOUNT
TOTAL	

RECEIVED BY ______________________

Receipt

Name	Date

DESCRIPTION OF ITEMS/SERVICE	AMOUNT
TOTAL	

RECEIVED BY ______________________

Receipt

Name	Date

DESCRIPTION OF ITEMS/SERVICE	AMOUNT
TOTAL	

RECEIVED BY ______________________

Receipt

Name	Date

DESCRIPTION OF ITEMS/SERVICE	AMOUNT
TOTAL	

RECEIVED BY ______________________

Receipt

Name	Date

DESCRIPTION OF ITEMS/SERVICE	AMOUNT
TOTAL	

RECEIVED BY ______________________

Receipt

Name	Date

DESCRIPTION OF ITEMS/SERVICE	AMOUNT
TOTAL	

RECEIVED BY ______________________

Receipt

Name	Date

DESCRIPTION OF ITEMS/SERVICE	AMOUNT
TOTAL	

RECEIVED BY ______________________

Receipt

Name	Date

DESCRIPTION OF ITEMS/SERVICE	AMOUNT
TOTAL	

RECEIVED BY ______________________________

Receipt

Name	Date

DESCRIPTION OF ITEMS/SERVICE	AMOUNT
TOTAL	

RECEIVED BY ______________________________

Receipt

Name	Date

DESCRIPTION OF ITEMS/SERVICE	AMOUNT
TOTAL	

RECEIVED BY ______________________________

Receipt

Name	Date

DESCRIPTION OF ITEMS/SERVICE	AMOUNT
TOTAL	

RECEIVED BY ______________________

Receipt

Name	Date

DESCRIPTION OF ITEMS/SERVICE	AMOUNT
TOTAL	

RECEIVED BY ______________________

Receipt

Name	Date

DESCRIPTION OF ITEMS/SERVICE	AMOUNT
TOTAL	

RECEIVED BY ______________________

Receipt

Name	Date

DESCRIPTION OF ITEMS/SERVICE	AMOUNT
TOTAL	

RECEIVED BY ______________________

Receipt

Name	Date

DESCRIPTION OF ITEMS/SERVICE	AMOUNT
TOTAL	

RECEIVED BY ______________________

Receipt

Name	Date

DESCRIPTION OF ITEMS/SERVICE	AMOUNT
TOTAL	

RECEIVED BY ______________________

Receipt

Name	Date

DESCRIPTION OF ITEMS/SERVICE	AMOUNT
TOTAL	

RECEIVED BY ____________________

Receipt

Name	Date

DESCRIPTION OF ITEMS/SERVICE	AMOUNT
TOTAL	

RECEIVED BY ____________________

Receipt

Name	Date

DESCRIPTION OF ITEMS/SERVICE	AMOUNT
TOTAL	

RECEIVED BY ____________________

Receipt

Name	Date

DESCRIPTION OF ITEMS/SERVICE	AMOUNT
TOTAL	

RECEIVED BY ______________________

Receipt

Name	Date

DESCRIPTION OF ITEMS/SERVICE	AMOUNT
TOTAL	

RECEIVED BY ______________________

Receipt

Name	Date

DESCRIPTION OF ITEMS/SERVICE	AMOUNT
TOTAL	

RECEIVED BY ______________________

Receipt

Name	Date

DESCRIPTION OF ITEMS/SERVICE	AMOUNT
TOTAL	

RECEIVED BY ______________________

Receipt

Name	Date

DESCRIPTION OF ITEMS/SERVICE	AMOUNT
TOTAL	

RECEIVED BY ______________________

Receipt

Name	Date

DESCRIPTION OF ITEMS/SERVICE	AMOUNT
TOTAL	

RECEIVED BY ______________________

Receipt

Name	Date

DESCRIPTION OF ITEMS/SERVICE	AMOUNT
TOTAL	

RECEIVED BY ______________________

Receipt

Name	Date

DESCRIPTION OF ITEMS/SERVICE	AMOUNT
TOTAL	

RECEIVED BY ______________________

Receipt

Name	Date

DESCRIPTION OF ITEMS/SERVICE	AMOUNT
TOTAL	

RECEIVED BY ______________________

Receipt

Name	Date

DESCRIPTION OF ITEMS/SERVICE	AMOUNT
TOTAL	

RECEIVED BY ______________________

Receipt

Name	Date

DESCRIPTION OF ITEMS/SERVICE	AMOUNT
TOTAL	

RECEIVED BY ______________________

Receipt

Name	Date

DESCRIPTION OF ITEMS/SERVICE	AMOUNT
TOTAL	

RECEIVED BY ______________________

Receipt

Name	Date

DESCRIPTION OF ITEMS/SERVICE	AMOUNT
TOTAL	

RECEIVED BY ______________________________

Receipt

Name	Date

DESCRIPTION OF ITEMS/SERVICE	AMOUNT
TOTAL	

RECEIVED BY ______________________________

Receipt

Name	Date

DESCRIPTION OF ITEMS/SERVICE	AMOUNT
TOTAL	

RECEIVED BY ______________________________

Receipt

Name	Date

DESCRIPTION OF ITEMS/SERVICE	AMOUNT
TOTAL	

RECEIVED BY ______________________

Receipt

Name	Date

DESCRIPTION OF ITEMS/SERVICE	AMOUNT
TOTAL	

RECEIVED BY ______________________

Receipt

Name	Date

DESCRIPTION OF ITEMS/SERVICE	AMOUNT
TOTAL	

RECEIVED BY ______________________

Receipt

Name	Date

DESCRIPTION OF ITEMS/SERVICE	AMOUNT
TOTAL	

RECEIVED BY ______________________

Receipt

Name	Date

DESCRIPTION OF ITEMS/SERVICE	AMOUNT
TOTAL	

RECEIVED BY ______________________

Receipt

Name	Date

DESCRIPTION OF ITEMS/SERVICE	AMOUNT
TOTAL	

RECEIVED BY ______________________

Receipt

Name	Date

DESCRIPTION OF ITEMS/SERVICE	AMOUNT
TOTAL	

RECEIVED BY ______________________

Receipt

Name	Date

DESCRIPTION OF ITEMS/SERVICE	AMOUNT
TOTAL	

RECEIVED BY ______________________

Receipt

Name	Date

DESCRIPTION OF ITEMS/SERVICE	AMOUNT
TOTAL	

RECEIVED BY ______________________

Receipt

Name	Date

DESCRIPTION OF ITEMS/SERVICE	AMOUNT
TOTAL	

RECEIVED BY ______________________

Receipt

Name	Date

DESCRIPTION OF ITEMS/SERVICE	AMOUNT
TOTAL	

RECEIVED BY ______________________

Receipt

Name	Date

DESCRIPTION OF ITEMS/SERVICE	AMOUNT
TOTAL	

RECEIVED BY ______________________

Receipt

Name	Date

DESCRIPTION OF ITEMS/SERVICE	AMOUNT
TOTAL	

RECEIVED BY ______________________

Receipt

Name	Date

DESCRIPTION OF ITEMS/SERVICE	AMOUNT
TOTAL	

RECEIVED BY ______________________

Receipt

Name	Date

DESCRIPTION OF ITEMS/SERVICE	AMOUNT
TOTAL	

RECEIVED BY ______________________

Receipt

Name	Date

DESCRIPTION OF ITEMS/SERVICE	AMOUNT
TOTAL	

RECEIVED BY ______________________________

Receipt

Name	Date

DESCRIPTION OF ITEMS/SERVICE	AMOUNT
TOTAL	

RECEIVED BY ______________________________

Receipt

Name	Date

DESCRIPTION OF ITEMS/SERVICE	AMOUNT
TOTAL	

RECEIVED BY ______________________________

Receipt

Name	Date

DESCRIPTION OF ITEMS/SERVICE	AMOUNT
TOTAL	

RECEIVED BY ______________________

Receipt

Name	Date

DESCRIPTION OF ITEMS/SERVICE	AMOUNT
TOTAL	

RECEIVED BY ______________________

Receipt

Name	Date

DESCRIPTION OF ITEMS/SERVICE	AMOUNT
TOTAL	

RECEIVED BY ______________________

Receipt

Name	Date

DESCRIPTION OF ITEMS/SERVICE	AMOUNT
TOTAL	

RECEIVED BY ______________________

Receipt

Name	Date

DESCRIPTION OF ITEMS/SERVICE	AMOUNT
TOTAL	

RECEIVED BY ______________________

Receipt

Name	Date

DESCRIPTION OF ITEMS/SERVICE	AMOUNT
TOTAL	

RECEIVED BY ______________________

Receipt

Name	Date

DESCRIPTION OF ITEMS/SERVICE	AMOUNT
TOTAL	

RECEIVED BY ______________________

Receipt

Name	Date

DESCRIPTION OF ITEMS/SERVICE	AMOUNT
TOTAL	

RECEIVED BY ______________________

Receipt

Name	Date

DESCRIPTION OF ITEMS/SERVICE	AMOUNT
TOTAL	

RECEIVED BY ______________________

Receipt

Name	Date

DESCRIPTION OF ITEMS/SERVICE	AMOUNT
TOTAL	

RECEIVED BY ______________________

Receipt

Name	Date

DESCRIPTION OF ITEMS/SERVICE	AMOUNT
TOTAL	

RECEIVED BY ______________________

Receipt

Name	Date

DESCRIPTION OF ITEMS/SERVICE	AMOUNT
TOTAL	

RECEIVED BY ______________________

Receipt

Name	Date

DESCRIPTION OF ITEMS/SERVICE	AMOUNT
TOTAL	

RECEIVED BY ______________________

Receipt

Name	Date

DESCRIPTION OF ITEMS/SERVICE	AMOUNT
TOTAL	

RECEIVED BY ______________________

Receipt

Name	Date

DESCRIPTION OF ITEMS/SERVICE	AMOUNT
TOTAL	

RECEIVED BY ______________________

Receipt

Name	Date

DESCRIPTION OF ITEMS/SERVICE	AMOUNT
TOTAL	

RECEIVED BY ______________________

Receipt

Name	Date

DESCRIPTION OF ITEMS/SERVICE	AMOUNT
TOTAL	

RECEIVED BY ______________________

Receipt

Name	Date

DESCRIPTION OF ITEMS/SERVICE	AMOUNT
TOTAL	

RECEIVED BY ______________________

Receipt

Name	Date

DESCRIPTION OF ITEMS/SERVICE	AMOUNT
TOTAL	

RECEIVED BY ______________________

Receipt

Name	Date

DESCRIPTION OF ITEMS/SERVICE	AMOUNT
TOTAL	

RECEIVED BY ______________________

Receipt

Name	Date

DESCRIPTION OF ITEMS/SERVICE	AMOUNT
TOTAL	

RECEIVED BY ______________________

Receipt

Name	Date

DESCRIPTION OF ITEMS/SERVICE	AMOUNT
TOTAL	

RECEIVED BY ______________________________

Receipt

Name	Date

DESCRIPTION OF ITEMS/SERVICE	AMOUNT
TOTAL	

RECEIVED BY ______________________________

Receipt

Name	Date

DESCRIPTION OF ITEMS/SERVICE	AMOUNT
TOTAL	

RECEIVED BY ______________________________

Receipt

Name	Date

DESCRIPTION OF ITEMS/SERVICE	AMOUNT
TOTAL	

RECEIVED BY ______________________

Receipt

Name	Date

DESCRIPTION OF ITEMS/SERVICE	AMOUNT
TOTAL	

RECEIVED BY ______________________

Receipt

Name	Date

DESCRIPTION OF ITEMS/SERVICE	AMOUNT
TOTAL	

RECEIVED BY ______________________

Receipt

Name	Date

DESCRIPTION OF ITEMS/SERVICE	AMOUNT
TOTAL	

RECEIVED BY ______________________________

Receipt

Name	Date

DESCRIPTION OF ITEMS/SERVICE	AMOUNT
TOTAL	

RECEIVED BY ______________________________

Receipt

Name	Date

DESCRIPTION OF ITEMS/SERVICE	AMOUNT
TOTAL	

RECEIVED BY ______________________________

Receipt

Name	Date

DESCRIPTION OF ITEMS/SERVICE	AMOUNT
TOTAL	

RECEIVED BY ___________________________

Receipt

Name	Date

DESCRIPTION OF ITEMS/SERVICE	AMOUNT
TOTAL	

RECEIVED BY ___________________________

Receipt

Name	Date

DESCRIPTION OF ITEMS/SERVICE	AMOUNT
TOTAL	

RECEIVED BY ___________________________

Receipt

Name	Date

DESCRIPTION OF ITEMS/SERVICE	AMOUNT
TOTAL	

RECEIVED BY ________________________

Receipt

Name	Date

DESCRIPTION OF ITEMS/SERVICE	AMOUNT
TOTAL	

RECEIVED BY ________________________

Receipt

Name	Date

DESCRIPTION OF ITEMS/SERVICE	AMOUNT
TOTAL	

RECEIVED BY ________________________

www.ingramcontent.com/pod-product-compliance
Lightning Source LLC
LaVergne TN
LVHW080000210926
848481LV00012B/3638